Tales of Old Kent

Alan Bignell

With Illustrations by Don Osmond

D1136885

COUNTRYSIDE BOOKS

NEWBURY, BERKSHIRE

First published 1986
© Alan Bignell 1986
Reprinted 1989, 1992, 1999, 2001, 2004, 2007

COUNTRYSIDE BOOKS
3 Catherine Road
Newbury, Berkshire

To view our complete range of books,
please visit us at
www.countrysidebooks.co.uk

ISBN 978 0 905392 75 2

Produced through MRM Associates Ltd., Reading
Printed by Cambridge University Press

*All material for the manufacture of this book
was sourced from sustainable forests.*

Other counties in this series include:

Buckinghamshire
Cambridgeshire
Cornwall
Cumbria
Derbyshire
Devon
Essex
Hampshire
Lancashire
Lincolnshire
Middlesex
Northamptonshire
Northumberland
Oxfordshire
Somerset
Staffordshire
Warwickshire
Wiltshire
North Yorkshire

Contents

CONTENTS

KENT – The map overleaf is by John Speede and shows the county as it was in the early seventeenth century.

Anne Boleyn
at Hever

T HE castle at Hever was a-bustle again. Sir Thomas Bullen
(only later to change the spelling of his family name
to the more courtly Boleyn) paced the courtyard, glancing
anxiously up now and again at the ramparts where a look-
out trumpeter kept watch.

King Henry VIII had taken to arriving at Hever at short
notice. Everyone knew, although he had said nothing himself,
that he was courting Sir Thomas' youngest daughter, Anne.
Nobody at that time could have foreseen the tragedy which
the Royal passion would bring upon Anne and the whole of
her family.

Most other young women of her day would have understood
the Royal intentions and been sufficiently flattered by them to
succumb. Anne's own sister, Mary, had already done so,
although her day as favourite of the Royal Bedchamber was
over now.

But Anne was not like other young women of her day. She
was not conventionally beautiful, although she was attractive,
with long dark hair and a vivacious wit. She was a great tease,
too, although it was whispered that she was incapable of
normal womanly emotions in the company of men. Today, she
would have been said to have been under-sexed if not actually
frigid. There were even those who whispered that she was a
witch.

When the Royal visits to Hever began she had good reason for not wishing to be polite to the king. His roving eye had first fallen upon Anne when she was lady in waiting to the queen, Katherine of Aragon. At that time, she had become secretly engaged to the Earl of Northumberland's young heir, Lord Harry Percy and when the king learned of it he angrily banished her from court and sent her home to Hever. When he came to visit her there, she showed her spirited displeasure by remaining in her room and sending down her excuses for not joining His Majesty and her parents.

Even when she finally deigned to leave her room during one of his visits and, after that, walked and rode with him in the gardens and park at Hever, she continued to dally with his undisguised ardour. She enchanted him with her gaiety, teased him with her flirtatiousness, even, as time went on, permitted him to take some liberties with her. What she would not allow, however, was the one thing the king most wanted from her.

'I will be queen – or I will be nothing,' she told him. The king was already married to his Queen Katherine, but he wanted Anne, and even more important, he wanted a male heir which Katherine had so far not been able to produce for him.

The king showered gifts and honours upon Anne and upon her father. He was a grasping old rascal and probably recognised the value to himself of his daughter's game of hard-to-get.

Eventually, Anne gave in to the king's relentless advances and was recalled to the court where neither of them took any trouble to disguise the relationship that was between them.

Henry now began to be increasingly impatient with Katherine as she, backed by the Church and the Pope, its Head, refused to allow him to have their marriage annulled, thus preventing his marrying Anne and fulfilling her Queen-or-nothing ultimatum, as well as hopefully producing the longed-for son and heir.

Henry sent Katherine away from court and treated Anne

more and more as though they were already married. It was she, and not the queen, who went with Henry on a visit to Calais and it was probably during that visit that she became pregnant.

Henry convinced himself that Anne's child would be the son he craved and he was determined that he should be legitimate, so that there could be no quibbling about the succession to the throne when the time came. The king and Anne were secretly married early one January morning in 1533, and ignored a Papal declaration that his marriage to Katherine was legal. Henry's own ministers found reasons to declare it null and void.

Anne was duly crowned Queen. It was not a popular coronation. Many people sympathised with Katherine, who refused to give up the title of Queen. The treasonable belief that Anne was a witch who had seduced the king and was responsible for the rift between Church and State, became more widespread than ever.

Henry then made it illegal for anyone not to accept Anne as Queen, and in a move which had huge consequences for the Church in England, he created the Church of England with himself as its head in place of the Pope. He thus became the authority for deciding on matters such as divorce. Equally valuable to the Crown was that he became responsible for the vast, vast wealth of the church in this country at that time. He ended all payments to Rome and imposed new taxes of his own instead.

Henry remained a Catholic and would perhaps have been content to have the country remain a member of the Roman Catholic church, but only on his own terms, which included recognition of Anne as his legal wife. Now, failure to recognise Henry as supreme Head of the church became a treasonable offence.

When that recognition was not forthcoming from most of the great monastic orders of the land, he dissolved the orders, executed their principals, and confiscated their lands and their wealth.

Anne's child was born on Sunday, September 7th, 1533, but it was not the son she and Henry had both hoped for. In fact, it was a girl which they called Elizabeth, who was destined to become the best-loved of all England's monarchs.

Henry was disappointed, but not despairing. Despair began to set in after Anne's next three pregnancies ended in miscarriages. Henry found himself falling out of love with his second wife. He blamed her for the necessity to which he was put of punishing men who served him well for their treasonable denial of the Act of Supremacy.

He found comfort with new mistresses and soon his loyal servants accused Anne of adultery with several men, including her own brother. Adultery by a queen was a treasonable offence, and so Anne was committed to the Tower in 1536, leaving Henry free to indulge his new passion for Jane Seymour.

As it became clear that the king had already made up his mind that Jane should be his next queen, public sympathy swung towards Anne, whose future now looked bleak. Anne was tried, found guilty and sentenced to death, as were the five men with whom she was alleged to have committed adultery.

Before her death, in an ironic move, she was forced to agree that her marriage to Henry had never been legal! This was said to be because of her prior contract to marry Lord Harry Percy, which Henry had forbidden. That agreement made her daughter, Elizabeth, illegitimate and ineligible to succeed to the throne instead of Jane's newly-born son.

The necessary agreement having been made, a swordsman was brought specially from Calais to execute Anne as deftly as possible. She went to her death with a composure and dignity that impressed everyone.

As soon as Henry heard Anne was dead, he stepped into the royal barge, dressed all in white, and was rowed down the Thames to where Jane Seymour waited for him. They were married at Hampton Court next day, May 30th, 1536, and in October of that year Jane bore Henry his longed for son.

14

Anne's father was ruined by the scandal and he died a broken man. He lies buried in Hever church, but his daughter, Anne, was buried within the Tower precincts, although she may have been disinterred and reburied in Norfolk some time later.

However that may be, it is Hever Castle she is said to haunt, no doubt reliving the happy days of her youth which were spent there, before a king lost his heart to her and she her head to him.

Pocahontas

GRAVESEND is a Thames-side town which for centuries has been the place where shipping bound for or leaving the London docks has stopped to take aboard or put ashore river pilots.

Today it is still a bustling place, with many interesting features, few of which arouse more interest, especially among North American visitors, than the statue of a Red Indian girl in deerskins, with a single feather in her headband.

It stands in the churchyard of St George's Church and it is the memorial to Princess Pocahontas, who came to England from Virginia in 1616 and died here before she could return to her native land less than a year later.

Although the statue is in Kent, most of her romantic story unfolded in America. It began in April 1607, when three ships of the newly-formed Virginia Company of London sailed into Chesapeake Bay. Aboard one of them was Captain John Smith, who had been one of the leaders of the expedition when it left England but who had lost some of his popularity en route.

The settlers set up the tents from which was to grow Jamestown, and it was from there that some of the men set out to explore. Smith, an ex-soldier, was among them.

At first the natives they encountered welcomed them, but later they attacked the foreigners and Smith was captured and taken before a chief of the Virginian Indians called Powhatan. He found himself in a long hut, where a fire blazed in the

16

middle. Powhatan sat on a dais at one end, surrounded by his wives, his children and his guards.

One of the women came forward and held a basin of water for Smith to wash himself and then he was made to sit down and take part in a feast that had been prepared for him. While he ate, the Indians decided among themselves how their victim should die.

Smith tried to keep his mind off whatever was to come. He looked round at the faces of the children and one pretty little girl caught his eye. He managed a smile and she returned his smile.

At last the meal was over and at its end Smith was seized and thrown down full length upon the ground, his head on a great stone which two of the men had rolled to the centre of the floor, very close to the fire which felt as though it would scorch his face.

Smith glanced up and saw two Indians standing over him, their faces tense with excitement, their arms raised, holding stone-headed tomahawks.

Smith had no doubt that he was living out his last few moments. But then, suddenly, something soft and warm fell on top of him, and Smith saw that it was the naked body of the

17

pretty little girl who had returned his smile. The girl was Pocahontas, daughter of Powhatan.

'He is mine!' the girl shouted. 'I take him. I am old enough and I want him.'

For a long moment no-one moved; no-one spoke. In the smokey silence in the hut Powhatan considered. At last the chief nodded.

'Very well,' he decided. The stone tomahawks were lowered and the executioners moved away. Pocahontas picked herself up and so did Smith. At once the mood of the Indians changed. From being sullenly expectant and broodingly excited, they became instantly jubilant and crowded round their reprieved prisoner, touching him and patting him and doing everything they knew to let him see how much their chief's decision delighted them.

From that moment, Smith was accepted as an honorary member of the chief's family. Despite her claim, Pocahontas was too young yet to be married to the Englishman, but nevertheless she had claimed him and he was made to understand that, when the right time came, he was to be her husband, and a full member of the tribe.

That night, instead of entering Paradise by way of a blood-spattered slab, he smoked the peace pipe with Powhatan and sat with the little naked Pocahontas on his knee until she fell asleep and was carried away to her bed by one of the women.

Pocahontas had fallen in love with the heavily-built, bearded Englishman and meant to marry him as soon as she was old enough. But in the meantime, her father had other plans for Smith. After a little while he sent him back to Jamestown with orders to bring back some of the cannons with which the Europeans had beaten off earlier Indian attacks.

When Smith reached the settlement, however, he found it peopled by starving and desperately ill survivors, and instead of returning to the Indians as he had promised, he stayed to help his own countrymen.

Pocahontas, realising that her man was not coming back to her, went to him instead. She was in love, not only with the man but also with the pictures of England that his stories had painted in her mind. She longed to go to England and see this place of wonders for herself. Smith was her only means of getting there.

But when she reached Jamestown, she learned that Smith had been badly injured in a gunpowder explosion and, near to death, had been taken aboard an English ship which had already sailed for home. Word reached the Indians that he had died and Pocahontas mourned her loss, though she did not lose her longing to see England.

Her friendliness towards the Englishmen led her into a trap and she was taken to Jamestown as a hostage for the future good behaviour of her father's people. However, she was sixteen years old and not an altogether unwilling hostage. She was well treated and made friends with some English girls of about her own age. She allowed herself to be clothed in English clothes and she learned lessons and was christened with the name Rebecca.

Soon after the departure of the ship that carried Smith back to England, another ship arrived with more settlers. Among them was a recently bereaved husband and father called John Rolfe. He was specially interested in growing tobacco, which was something the Indian girl knew about because she and her family had been growing tobacco for generations. She took a keen interest in his work and, with her help, Rolfe produced good crops and was soon shipping back to England the first of the English-grown Virginia tobacco.

Working together as they did, Rolfe fell in love with Pocahontas and eventually they were married. They had a son, who they called Tom.

In 1616 Rolfe decided they should visit England and, together with some other Indians, they sailed for London. The Indians were the first to arrive in England from the New World and they aroused a great deal of interest, especially

Pocahontas who was accepted as a Princess and entertained by King James I and his queen, Anne, at the Court Christmas revels.

Pocahontas learned to dance and also to ride a horse, and she saw all the tourist sights of her day: the Tower of London and its famous menagerie being one of the foremost. She met many famous people, too, including Sir Walter Raleigh, by now an old man, and Ben Johnson.

But although London excited her with its strangeness, it tired her with its noise and its activity and she found the cobbled streets very hard on feet that, until a few years ago, had never known anything but forest floors and grassy banks beneath their bare soles. She much preferred Norfolk, where she and Rolfe spent some time visiting his family.

But, all too soon for her, they were back in London again, where the cold damp atmosphere began to take its toll of her health.

It was while she was recovering from one of a series of bouts of illness that she met again the first Englishman she had loved, and whose life she had saved, John Smith.

He was now thirty-seven. She had learned when she arrived in England that he was not dead as she had believed, and she was such a celebrity that he could not have failed to know of her presence in London almost as soon as she arrived. Yet he had not bothered to seek her out until now, eight months later.

The woman, married to a good man and mother of his child, knew that the girlish passion that had sent her sprawling naked across his helpless body had not been real love. She saw Smith now for what he was: an ageing braggart and a self-seeking adventurer. She had no regrets that it had been her marriage to Rolfe, not Smith, that had brought her to this London she had so fervently longed to see.

Poor Pocahontas. Neither the city nor the man who had aroused her desire to see it had fulfilled her expectations. Wearied with illness and disillusioned, she wanted nothing so much now as to go home to her own beloved Virginia. But her illness was already too far advanced. By the time she and

Rolfe were ready to leave London aboard a ship called *The George*, to sail back to America, Pocahontas was so weak she had to be carried aboard.

It was clear to all that she was dying. It was her wish that their son should remain in England to be brought up as an Englishman, and so he was. Both Countess Mountbatten of Burma and Nancy, Lady Astor are said to have been among his descendants.

Before the ship left the Thames, the Indian princess was dead. At Gravesend, she was carried ashore and was buried in the church by the riverside. Her husband went back across the Atlantic without her, widowed for the second time.

It was not until 1958 that the bronze statue – the twin of one already in Jamestown and the gift of the people of Virginia, USA – was erected to her memory. The actual site of her grave is unknown, but the memorial, standing today in the churchyard garden, is very much a part of Kent's own heritage. The story of Pocahontas, the North American Princess who saved the life of the Englishman she loved and lost her own life in his country, is one of the most poignant of all the tales of Old Kent.

The Goodwin Sands

ENGLAND may never have known quite such a terrible storm, before or since, as that which swept across the country in November 1703. It lasted altogether for almost two weeks, during which it was said that in Kent alone a thousand homes and barns were blown flat.

But it was at sea that the worst loss of life occurred and even the gluttony of the notorious Goodwin Sands, the infamous 'shippe swallower' four miles off the Kentish coast at Deal, was sated for once.

The Goodwin Sands are, in fact, a series of sandbanks whose very origins are part of Kent lore, for it is said they were once the fertile acres of the ancient Island of Lomea. According to legend, the Island was lost to the sea because of the neglect of the 11th century Earl Godwin, part of whose Kentish estates it was.

Throughout history the sands have chilled seamen with their reputation for devouring whole ships, often in a matter of a few hours, and for constantly shifting so that they almost seem to be on the prowl for unwary vessels and their crews.

Yet, by acting as a huge natural breakwater, it is the Goodwins that have made The Downs a traditional safe refuge for Channel shipping in bad weather.

In 1703 a whole fleet of English warships under the command of Sir Cloudesley Shovel anchored in The Downs to ride out the unprecedented fury of the storm. But the wind, instead of abating, continued to increase in strength and at about one o'clock on the morning of November 27th several of the warships began to drag their anchors.

One by one the ships of the fleet were blown onto those lurking sands. *Northumberland*, a third-rater of seventy guns, was lost with all 253 of her crew. *Restoration* and *Stirling Castle* went down with her.

Mary, flying the flag of Rear-Admiral Beaumont, broke into pieces and was lost with all but one of her 272 men, including the admiral himself.

The only survivor, a seaman called Thomas Atkins, was washed off the vessel as she broke up and while he was in the water, clinging to a piece of timber, he saw the admiral leave the ship's quarter-deck and drown. Then a freak wave heaved Atkins bodily up onto the upper deck of the *Stirling Castle* as she plunged past on her way to her own doom, so that it was aboard her that he was shipwrecked for the second time that terrible night.

Once again he was hurled overboard as the sea pounded the trapped ship, and this time he fell into the one ship's boat that remained intact. In that, he was eventually buffeted ashore, almost unconscious from the effects of his ordeal, but destined to survive to tell his almost incredible tale.

There were no survivors from *Restoration*'s crew of 386.

Other ships cut their anchor chains and ran for the open sea which, though terrible enough, offered a better chance of survival than the relentless Goodwin Sands.

That storm claimed four major warships and 1,190 navy lives on the Goodwin Sands alone. In all, 13 ships and almost 2,000 officers and men were lost in that storm, the greatest number lost in either storm or battle in the history of the Royal Navy up to that time.

Of a hundred and sixty vessels at anchor in The Downs on November 26, only seventy remained afloat twenty-four hours later. The sea was littered with wreckage, including the upturned keels of several complete ships.

Violent storms have fed the Goodwin Sands their regular tribute of ships and human lives throughout history, and many strange stories have been told of ships and crews unfortunate enough to have fallen victim to the ship swallower.

Another story began with the wreck of the *Mahratta* in April 1909. She was the largest ship at that time ever to have succumbed to the Goodwins and she ran foul of them with a crew of ninety, seventeen passengers and ten thousand tons of tea, jute, rubber, rice and other cargo. Local men salvaged much of the cargo before tugs could arrive. They failed to pull the great ship free, and actually tore her apart in the attempt.

But the story did not end until more than thirty years later when, in October 1939, a second vessel called *Mahratta*, owned by the same company, was also wrecked on the Goodwin Sands, less than a mile from where her predecessor lay buried!

Another victim of the sands was the steamship *Montrose*, which won its own small niche in history as the ship upon which Dr Crippen and his mistress had travelled to Canada in 1910, when he became the first murderer to be caught by the use of wireless telegraphy.

In calm weather and at low tide, the Goodwin Sands can become a playground on which any number of unusual activities have been held, from games of cricket to bicycle races. But as soon as the tide begins to return, the sands lose their brief benevolence and become treacherous, clutching and unfriendly, ready to add to their collection of broken vessels and hapless seamen.

Hengist
and
Horsa

THE people of Kent like to claim that it was in their county
that the English nation emerged from the separate
groups that peopled Britain before the arrival of Hengist and
Horsa at Ebbsfleet in AD 449.

That arrival changed – indeed, for all practical purposes,
began – the history of England. Even legend is not very sure
where the men came from. One story hints at dark deeds in
the Saxon homelands of what is now northern Germany, with
a man called Horsa exiled after a dispute with his local
chieftain in which blood was spilled and lives were lost.

Another would have us believe that their arrival was
nothing more than one incident among many in a long and
spasmodic migration westward and southward across Northern Europe.

Certainly, Saxon raiders had been coming ashore since
before the Romans left Britain. In the very heyday of the
Roman colony, a Count of the Saxon Shore had had to be
appointed to mastermind defence of the whole south-east
coastline, from Norfolk round to Hampshire. Fortresses were
built to provide bases for the first organised coast guard.
Several of the later famous south-east ports began their active

26

service as bases for elements of the Roman fleet that had the special task of chasing off the northern pirates.

After the withdrawal of the legions, Britain was left to defend itself as best it could. This was not always terribly well. The unity that Rome had enforced broke down. Some of the local leaders attempted to fight off the raiders, others resorted to bribery, some put their faith optimistically in trading agreements. They were harrassed by many different invaders; mainly these were Picts who had begun to settle in northern Britain and Saxons who wished to live off the relative affluence of southern Britain.

The Saxons were not in any sense one nation, and they did not come specifically from the region we call Saxony today. The term Saxon is not very different from the term Indians as used by colonists to mean collectively the native nations of North America.

They were North-Eastern European adventurers, explorers, warriors and pirates who wrested a living from weaker neighbours by pillage and plunder.

In AD 449 the ruler of a kingdom that included all of modern Kent, much of East Anglia and more besides, was called Vortigern, and he found himself fighting off threats from the Picts in the north and Saxon pirates in the south and east. He could not fight both with any hope of beating either, so he resorted to diplomacy. He let it be known that he was in the market for a treaty with a mercenary force that would help him defend his kingdom in return for land on which they could settle permanently.

The so-called Saxons included two related groups, the Jutes and the Angles, and it was Horsa the Jute and his brother Hengist who sailed south with their three longships full of warriors to offer their martial services to Vortigern in return for their own piece of Britain. In fact, it was the Isle of Thanet that Vortigern offered them: in those days a true island off the north-eastern tip of Kent. It was here the Jutish brothers beached their craft when they first arrived.

They brought with them their own battle banner, a prancing white horse, and this proud family emblem flew over the new Jutish settlement on Thanet, where they made their homes. They sent for their families to farm the new land for them whilst they were fighting the Picts for Vortigern.

Soon the Isle of Thanet was too crowded for their liking, and Hengist and Horsa began to cast covetous eyes over some of the fertile mainland areas just across the Wantsum channel that made Thanet an island. They plotted to take the land from Vortigern.

The King had met and fallen in love with Hengist's daughter, Rowena, and he proposed that the two should be married. It would, of course, have been an acceptable bond between the two peoples, uniting them more firmly than their mutual bargain did. But in fact Hengist had, by this time, already worked out a more ambitious plan than mere absorption into the British lifestyle as father-in-law to a British king.

He pretended to favour the marriage and a date was set for the wedding. It brought with it the traditional feasting without which no Royal nuptials could be regarded as properly concluded, and when the bride's father and other relatives arrived to join in the celebrations they were welcomed by Vortigern and his court. The Britons were ostentatiously unarmed for the occasion. The Jutes, however, were only ostensibly unarmed. At a suitable moment during the jollifications, the Jutes drew daggers and swords and fell upon their hosts in an orgy of bloodletting.

Vortigern and his son Catigern managed to escape with their lives, and the Jutes proclaimed themselves masters of the kingdom.

That was not the end of the matter, of course. Vortigern did not just accept involuntary exile. He gathered an army together and tried to take back what had been his. There were several battles, none of which was more telling than the Battle of Aylesford on the river Medway, in which Horsa and Catigern killed each other in single combat and after which Hengist declared himself King of Kent.

There were other battles; some the Britons won, some the Saxons, but Vortigern never regained his realm. After Aylesford, Hengist had more land than he could use and he sent home for more settlers to come and join him. Those that came, however, were from another part of the Saxon homelands and were a different, although related, people. They settled in the newly won lands west of the river Medway, while the original settlers built up their estates on the eastern side.

It was that separation that began the surviving tradition of a divided Kent, with the Men of Kent residing in East Kent and the Kentish Men on the west side of the river.

Kent thus became the first part of Britain to be united under Saxon rule and since it was the Saxons, of whom the Angles emerged as the dominant group, who gradually edged the Celts westward and established the English nation, Kent claims to be the birthplace of that nationhood, where the prancing White Horse of Hengist and Horsa still flies, perhaps the most distinctive and easily recognised of all the county emblems of England.

The Ashes

IN the Pavilion at Lords is one of the most famous of all sporting trophies, The Ashes. It is the prize contested by the cricket teams of England and Australia, although regardless of which side wins a series, the little urn with its small handful of ashes never actually leaves the care of the Marylebone Cricket Club in England.

The Ashes are supposed to be those of a single wicket bail, symbolising England's success during a cricket tour Down Under.

But are they? Or is it possible that a little story associated with Cobham Hall, near Gravesend is true? It is a story that has been hinted at persistently down the years, and is now an established legend of cricketing history.

Cobham Hall is the family home of the Earls of Darnley, although currently it is owned by a trust, one of the administrators of which is the present earl, and is used as a private girls school.

There is no doubt about the origins of the urn itself. That was given to the Hon. Ivo Bligh, of Cobham Hall, in 1883 and it stayed at Cobham until 1927.

Ivo Bligh was an enthusiastic cricketer. He played in the Eton first XI and was a member of the 1878 Cambridge side which had an unbeaten record that included thrashing a visiting Australian team by an innings and 72 runs.

Unhappily, ill health cut short a splendid sporting career after Bligh had played for Kent from 1877 until 1883, during which period he was several times captain of the county side.

Even when his playing days were over, he was twice President of the Kent County Cricket Club, in 1892 and 1902, and he was also President of the MCC in 1900.

31

However, Ivo Bligh was still playing for Kent when, in August 1882, England lost to Australia at Kennington Oval for the first time in a home Test Match. It was a famous victory for the Australians and a defeat which England felt very keenly indeed. So much, in fact, that the *Sporting Times* mourned the occasion with a mock obituary notice which read: 'In affectionate remembrance of English cricket, which died at the Oval on 29th August 1882, deeply lamented by a large circle of sorrowing friends and acquaintances. RIP. NB – the body will be cremated and the Ashes taken to Australia.'

In fact, no ashes (with or without a capital A!) were actually taken to Australia. However, when later that year Ivo Bligh led a touring team down under, word went around England that he and his team had embarked upon a cricketing Crusade, the declared object of which was to bring back The Ashes.

The tour was a great success and if English cricket had died at the Oval it was revived somewhat in Australia. After three matches, the England side was 2-1 up and a group of Australian ladies ceremoniously burned one of the Test wicket bails and collected up the ashes which they put into a small pottery urn. The urn was presented to the captain of the England side, Ivo Bligh.

The gesture was, in fact, a bit premature because a fourth match was played which the Australians won, so the tour ended with a two games draw.

Nevertheless, the England side did bring back the Ashes. The little urn was placed in an honoured position on a mantelpiece at Cobham Hall and not long afterwards one of the ladies who had presented it to the England captain, a Miss Florence Morphy, followed it to England to become Ivo Bligh's wife.

In 1900 the Hon. Ivo Bligh succeeded to the family title and became the 8th Earl of Darnley.

That much is history. But legend has added its own curious little footnote to the story. It claims that one day, while a Cobham Hall maid was dusting the mantelpiece where the urn stood, she accidentally knocked it over. The precious Ashes spilled into the fireplace below, where a fire was burning, and were lost.

The poor girl was aghast. Whatever had she done? Luckily, the pottery urn was undamaged and she stood it up again and went on with her dusting, hoping that no-one would ever find out that the urn was now empty.

It was not, though, something she could just walk away from, as though it had never happened. Those were not just any old ashes she had lost for posterity. They were The Ashes – unique and in some English eyes at least, only very barely less precious than the Crown Jewels themselves.

She worried about it for the rest of the day and that evening, when she went home to her parents in the village, she told her father what had happened. He, it seems, was a pragmatic man, well aware that what was done could not be undone, though it could, perhaps, be made to seem as if it had not been done.

'There's only one thing you can do, my girl,' he told his daughter. 'Wood ash is wood ash, wherever it comes from. Next time you are in the room where the urn is, you scoop up a bit of wood ash from the fire and put that in the urn. No-one will ever know the difference.' And that – the story avers – is just what the girl did.

When Lord Darnley died, aged 68, in 1927, his widow presented the urn to the MCC, where it remains to this day. What nobody knows, though – not really *knows* for certain – is whether the ashes it contains are those of that bail burned in Australia more than a hundred years ago by a party of high-spirited young ladies, or nothing more than a handful of undistinguished firewood ash from a Cobham Hall fireplace.

Perhaps, on the whole, it would be best all round if no-one ever did know.

The Battle of Goudhurst

THE people of Goudhurst were well-drilled in what to do when the Hawkhurst Gang rode into town. The few townsfolk who were in the street ran for cover, scooping up children and bustling them indoors, where they lowered heavy wooden beams to secure the doors and closed solid timber shutters to protect their windows.

The gang would ride into the town, high-spirited, a little drunk, firing pistols into the air and galloping their horses through the narrow main street with wild whoops that scattered chickens and pigs in all directions.

During one visit from the gang a stranger to the town rode in at one end of the main street just as the gangsters began their madcap gallop from the other. He did not know what to do and had nowhere to go. He was engulfed, yanked from the saddle and thrown to the ground where he was kicked, beaten and robbed of what little money he carried, as well as his watch and a ring. Then he was left for dead where he lay.

He probably saved some of the townsfolk from a scarcely less violent fate, satisfying the gang's lust for plunder so that there was nothing to detain them. They rode off to convert their booty into liquor and the little Kentish town fell quiet again.

It sounds like something out of the American Wild West but it actually happened in 1747, in Kent's own Wild West, an area of what is known as the High Weald around the villages of Goudhurst and Hawkhurst.

The Hawkhurst Gang roamed freely throughout the south of England. Its exploits were reported as far apart as Poole in Dorset and the Isle of Sheppey in the Thames Estuary. The gangsters were smugglers, and among the first of their kind to make the trade into really big business, landing and distributing illicit cargoes worth many thousands of pounds at a time.

The profits from this trade were enormous and gang leaders could afford to pay their men more for one night's work with them than could be earned in a week by a farm labourer or village craftsman.

Of course, it was illegal and dangerous work. Excisemen, supported by troops of dragoons, sometimes laid ambushes, attacking smuggling gangs in an effort to drive them off, leaving their cargoes to be confiscated in the name of the Crown. But the cargoes were too valuable to abandon without a fight and while the recruits helped land the contraband and haul it inland to prepared hiding places, the smugglers formed armed escorts. If they were attacked, there was invariably a fight which the smugglers often won, frequently after several men on both sides had been killed and wounded.

Sometimes prisoners were taken and brought before local magistrates, who committed them to Sessions at Maidstone, knowing perfectly well that there was a strong probability that the farm carts in which the prisoners were transported would be intercepted, the escorting soldiers driven off and the men released. As often as not, the cart would be left a smouldering heap of wood ash in the road as well.

Many of the magistrates sympathised with the smugglers and some even had a financial stake in their activities. It was not unknown for soldiers and Excisemen who accused smugglers of wounding colleagues to find themselves facing charges of wounding the smugglers instead.

The Hawkhurst Gang made the Kent and Sussex border

village of Hawkhurst the capital of its own little kingdom, which it ruled with considerable savagery, exacting terrible vengeance from anyone who tried to stand against it. When there was no smuggling to be done, the gangsters spent their comparative wealth in inns and taverns. When their money was gone, they rode on drunken forays, taking at gunpoint food and anything else they wanted from farms and homes, or from any luckless travellers unfortunate enough to fall into their hands.

It was to this state of lawlessness that a young soldier called William Sturt returned home from the Army in 1747. He lived in the village of Goudhurst, some three miles from Hawkhurst, which was also the home of three of the Hawkhurst Gang's leaders, the Kingsmill brothers: Thomas, George and Richard.

Sturt had been a Corporal in the Army and had served abroad, including two years in Jamaica. When some of the Goudhurst villagers decided they had had enough of being bullied by the smugglers and began to talk of making a stand against them, it was perhaps natural that they should turn to Sturt to help them rid their village of the reign of terror under which it had suffered for so long.

Sturt agreed, and under his leadership Goudhurst formed its own militia with the avowed intention of making the village a no-go area for the gang.

The Kingsmill brothers soon heard about the formation of the Goudhurst Militia and decided at once that it could not be allowed to go unchallenged or other villages in their 'kingdom' would also be tempted to mount opposition to them.

So they kidnapped one of the militiamen and forced him to tell them its plans. After beating him up, they sent him back to the village with a message that they would ride into Goudhurst, a hundred strong, and plunder the town, murder all its inhabitants and burn it to the ground.

So sure were they that they would overcome the militia that they even announced the exact time and date on which they would arrive to do all this.

Sturt received the news and made preparations to meet

them. He sent men out to scour the countryside for guns, powder, and lead to melt into bullets. He received help from many of the local farmers who had suffered at the hands of the Hawkhurst Gang. These had no objections to the smuggling, which they regarded as the exercise of free trade, to which all Englishmen were entitled whatever the government of the day said about it. But they were no friends of the Hawkhurst Gang, who had thought nothing of commandeering horses and wagons when they needed them, returning them damaged and useless for farm work. Some farmers who had protested had had their ricks and barns burned.

In Goudhurst, parties were set to work digging trenches and raising barricades, and places were chosen for marksmen on rooftops. The church was made ready for use as a refuge for those women and children who could not be evacuated to friends and relatives within the surrounding countryside.

By the time the gang was due to begin its attack, all was ready, and the militiamen waited at their posts.

Exactly when they had said they would, on April 20th, 1747, the gang rode in, one hundred of them, bared to the waist in the morning sunshine and carrying long guns, pistols and cutlasses.

They were led by Thomas and Richard Kingsmill, and Richard made sure the townsfolk were under no illusions about what he intended for them. He stood up in his stirrups and shouted that before the morning was done he would broil four of the townsmen's hearts and eat them that night for supper.

Sturt ordered his men not to fire first but when the gangsters fired their first volley, the militiamen returned the fire and killed one attacker. In the short sharp battle that followed, two more of the gang were killed and several were wounded. One of those killed was Richard Kingsmill. The defenders suffered no casualties and, realising they had badly miscalculated, the remaining members of the gang turned and fled. The militiamen, flushed with victory, chased after them and several prisoners were taken.

It was the beginning of the end for the Hawkhurst Gang.

The other two Kingsmill brothers were arrested some time afterwards. They were tried, condemned and hanged. The gang did not break up immediately, but it was never as strong again and its hold over the High Weald villages was broken for ever.

William Sturt became Master of the Goudhurst Poor House and married a local girl called Ann Beeching. They both dropped out of history's notice after that, but there is no reason to suppose they did not live happily ever after in the best of story-book traditions.

Today, the village of Goudhurst is one of the most attractive in that part of Kent, and as law abiding and peaceful as any. But it does not forget that day, more than 250 years ago, when it took the law into its own hands and ended the reign of terror of the infamous Hawkhurst Gang.

Hoodening

N O-ONE knows what the origins of 'hoodening' are. There
are those who believe it began in Kent more than a
thousand years ago, when the Jutes brought their veneration
of the horse to these parts, and that the 'hooden horse' was
originally the Woden (or Odin) Horse that featured in some
ancient Saxon ritual.

Others favour the belief that the horse originated much
more recently as nothing more than the most threatening
'prop' available to groups of labourers who used it to help
extract gifts from neighbours at Christmas time.

But sometimes, even today, you will find at country fetes
and town fairs in Kent a group of dancers with a hooden
horse. They are not hoodeners in the original sense, but
Morris dancers who have introduced a traditional-style
hooden horse into their performances.

Until about 150 years ago, hoodening was as much a feature
of Christmas on the Isle of Thanet and some other parts of
East Kent as carols and cards are today. But by then none of
those who took part in it had any handed-on memory of how it
all began; it was used rather like the guy for which youngsters
solicit pennies for Bonfire Night.

The hooden horse itself was a wooden representation of a
horse's head, on a broomstick, with straw or rope for a mane
and a bit of sackcloth fastened to the neck and hanging loosely
over the pole to make a body.

The head was made with the lower jaw hinged to the upper
with a bit of leather in such a way that it could be moved up

and down with a length of string, to make the jaws clack together. To heighten the effect, the insides of the jaws were often lined with hobnails to represent teeth, so that when the jaws were, in fact, opened and shut again, the head made a fierce snapping sound which, together with the often fairly frightening appearance achieved by the painted eyes and flaring nostrils, could be quite terrifying, especially by candle or lamp light.

It was meant to be! A man would get under the sackcloth body and 'ride' the broomstick, like a child on a hobby-horse, jerking the jaw-string with one hand to make the jaws snap as he cavorted along. The rest of the little band of hooupeners included, traditionally, The Rider, who was for ever trying, always comically unsuccessfully, to mount the horse; the Waggoner, distinguished by his long waggoner's whip, which he cracked over the head of the horse; and The Molly, a man dressed as a woman, who fulfilled a role rather similar to that of a pantomime dame, and who bustled along behind the horse forever sweeping the ground vigorously with a besom broom.

The prancing of the horse always involved a good deal of kicking up of heels and snapping at the legs of any young ladies and the whole performance was often pretty rowdy, fairly bawdy and generally rather licentious.

The main characters would be accompanied by a group of whatever musicians could be recruited from the local talent and the whole band would set off to make the rounds of the village, the Waggoner leading the Horse from house to house, its teeth gnashing menacingly as gifts of cash or the traditional cakes and ale were requested noisily from the householders.

As time went by, the ceremony became more and more robust. As it began to get out of control it became a public nuisance. It is said that hoodening was banned entirely in Thanet early in the 19th century after one poor woman was scared literally to death by the horse.

But the hooden horse survived in other parts of East Kent and today it is cherished as one of the relics of a past when the horse was revered as a sacred symbol in the White Horse county of Kent.

The
Invicta Legend

INVICTA means 'Unconquered' and Kent has this word for its motto as a result of the stubborn resistance it showed towards the Norman army of William the Conqueror. It was a resistance which ended in honourable negotiation rather than the defeat and unconditional surrender forced upon the rest of England.

William earned his title of Conqueror at Hastings in 1066 and then travelled to London where he had set the crown upon his own head on Christmas Day of that year. In 1067 Saxon England waited anxiously to see what was going to happen to it now that it was Norman England.

Before the Norman invasion force had landed at Pevensey in Sussex the previous year it had tried to land at Romney in Kent, but had been beaten off by the local men. William did not forget that. As soon as he had defeated King Harold, he and his soldiers turned eastwards and demonstrated to the men of New Romney just what they thought of the welcome they had received from Kent.

Then, having taught New Romney a lesson by sword and by fire, William pressed on to Dover, whose menfolk were mostly still limping back from Hastings, leaving the town virtually undefended. There was a garrison at the castle, however, and that put up a good fight before it was overrun by the Normans. William decided that these obstinate Kentish Men were going to have to be taught another sharp lesson.

He had the castle commander, Bertram de Ashburnham, and his two sons beheaded in front of the rest of the garrison survivors, and then he set his followers loose on the defenceless town.

The Normans, with professional thoroughness, murdered and pillaged, plundered and looted, and finally set fire to whatever was left.

They went too far, in fact. William needed Dover. Even then, before the great stone castle reared up on top of The Heights, Dover was acknowledged to be the key to the kingdom. William could not claim to have vanquished England while resistance forces could still control the town and, more important, the Strait that was the weakest link in his line of communication and supply from Normandy.

He decided it would be diplomatic to show his displeasure with his men publicly, so instead of marching away and leaving Dover to literally smoulder behind him, he ordered his men to repair the castle earthworks and for a week he did what he could to try to persuade the people of Dover that Normans were not as bad as first impressions might have led them to suppose they were.

At last, though, they did march off, and entered London where the coronation took place amid scenes of violence and bloodshed and the burning of more homes.

But Kent was far from won over to William and the new king knew it. As soon as he could, he left London and led his followers south, intending to retake and this time to permanently occupy Dover Castle.

It was while they were marching through north west Kent, somewhere near Swanscombe, that the Normans saw coming towards them what at first looked like a forest on the march. It was an unnerving sight, and the Normans watched with some apprehension until, having completely surrounded the king's men, the forest stopped moving. Then, at a signal, the forest of green boughs was cast aside by the men that carried them, revealing an army of the Men of Kent, led by Archbishop Stigand and Abbot Egelsin, all heavily armed.

They told William that they came to offer him their allegiance if he would, in turn, grant them their ancient laws and privileges. Otherwise, they said, he could expect war – 'and that most deadly', to use the traditional words of the challengers.

There must have been a moment or two when William weighed up his chances of defeating this strange Kentish army. But he was no novice tactician and he must have seen all too clearly that there was a very good chance that he might be taught a thing or two himself if he took it on.

Even if he chose to fight, and won, there remained the very strong possibility that the victory might prove to be so expensive in Norman lives that other Saxons in other parts of the country might decide it was a good time to press claims of their own. He decided he had more to win by accepting the offer of peace.

The Men of Kent set forth their demands, which were, essentially, that they should be allowed to enjoy under Norman rule all those special rights and privileges granted to them by Edward the Confessor and his successors.

Naturally, William wanted to know just what rights and privileges they were and the Kentish Men named them, adding a few they had long felt sure the Confessor would have conferred upon them if he had ever got round to it and which, in any case, they were already in the habit of enjoying just as if he had.

William agreed. Why not, after all? He could always change his mind just as soon as he judged it was safe to do so. In return, he made it a condition that Dover Castle should be officially surrendered to him.

The Kentish Men had expected that. But then, what use was the castle to them, now that the latest threat had outflanked it?

There was a general agreement, and the two sides went away from the encounter well pleased with themselves.

That was how Kent came to keep many of its old Saxon traditions, including the old Jutish law of succession to property, known as *gavelkind*, which allowed owners of estates in Kent to continue to bequeath property to be shared among all their sons and daughters, while the Norman practice of handing property down to the eldest son was adopted elsewhere.

For centuries, estate owners in Kent had to have a special Act of Parliament to allow them to be succeeded by their eldest sons, and that was legally the case until *gavelkind* was abolished by Act of Parliament as recently as 1925.

Today, a commemorative stone at Swanscombe recalls that historic meeting between the 'moving forest' of camouflaged Men of Kent and King William I – the meeting that allowed the county to claim as its motto the one proud word *Invicta*, Unconquered, because they alone of all the men of all the counties of England had not been conquered by William, but had, instead, negotiated an honourable partnership.

Wat Tyler
and the
Royal Kiss

THE peasants revolt of June 1381 is usually spoken of as the Wat Tyler rebellion, and Wat Tyler is usually thought to have been a tiler by trade from Dartford in Kent.

There is no doubt at all that it did take place, that it involved men from Kent, as well as from Essex and other Home Counties, and that apart from creating some variety in the lives of people who normally had to content themselves with such standards of excitement as were set by the annual fair on the village green, it achieved very little indeed.

Tradition has it that the revolt was sparked off when a poll tax collector overstepped the bounds of acceptable zeal by trying to establish whether or not Tyler's daughter was old enough to be taxed. It was said that when the man tried to crudely reveal what he chose to regard as the material evidence for his claim that the girl definitely was old enough, Tyler struck him with one of the tools of his trade and killed him.

Whether or not that is literally true, what is significant is that it happened at a time of relative prosperity for the labouring classes in England. There was plenty of work, mainly because the population had been so drastically

46

reduced by the Black Death which by this time had run its course, and so wages were relatively high. These conditions had bred an air of independence among labourers throughout the country. The ruling classes had then felt obliged to react by asserting their own rights more and more harshly.

From 1359 to 1371 Englishmen had paid no direct taxes. When the King's ministers added to their unpopularity by levying the new poll tax, widespread discontent built up, especially in the most populated and therefore most heavily taxed south-eastern counties. It needed only some small incident to spark off revolt and riot.

Whatever that incident was, a rebellious mob marched from the Thames-side towns of Dartford and Gravesend and from the surrounding villages, first to Rochester and then to Maidstone.

At Rochester they captured the castle, freed prisoners from its dungeons and recruited more malcontents to swell their numbers. It was at Maidstone that they chose Wat Tyler as their spokesman and leader, and it was under his leadership that they marched on Canterbury where they hoped to find Archbishop Sudbury, who was the king's Chancellor and therefore the man who had introduced the hated poll tax.

The rebels may not have been all that surprised that His Grace was nowhere to be found. But by this time they were thoroughly roused and had no intention of simply shrugging their shoulders and going home. The now sizeable army of rebels turned and began to march on London.

Their way took them through Maidstone again, where this time they stormed the Archbishop's prison from which they freed a priest, John Ball, who had been preaching a kind of socialism that had lost him his liberty and endangered his life.

Ball marched with the rebels from Maidstone to Blackheath, outside London, and there he preached his most famous sermon, using as his text the revolutionary couplet: 'When Adam delved and Eve span, Who was then the Gentleman?'

The thought behind this little rhyme was that when Adam

and Eve had dug (delved) and spun (span) in the Garden of Eden, there had been no 'gentlemen' to lord it over them and skim off the fruits of their labour in taxes to support their own idleness. It was a philosophy dear to the hearts of the peasants, who cheered the sermon to the echo.

While the mob was camped on Blackheath, deciding what to do next, the king's mother, Joan, known as the Fair Maid of Kent, arrived. She was said to be among the most beautiful women in the world and was as popular in her day as, say, the late Diana, Princess of Wales, became in hers. She was on her way back to London from a pilgrimage to Canterbury, and she had to cross the heath which meant passing through the rebel encampment.

Many a woman in her position would have turned back, but not Joan, and when the rebels learned who it was that had come among them, they thronged around. Many of them believed she could be relied upon to advise her fourteen year old son, King Richard II, more wisely than his ministers had been doing – which, in effect, meant they expected her to persuade the king to accede to the rebels' demands.

The Queen Mother wanted to know what all the fuss was about and Wat Tyler stepped forward to explain. He asked her to speak to the king on their behalf, and she promised to do that. Then she asked to be allowed to go on her way without molestation and Tyler, buoyed up with the success of their venture so far and a bit carried away by the excitement of the moment, told her that she might have safe passage through their ranks if she would give him a kiss first.

Joan was shrewd as well as beautiful. Quite how she felt about the proposal we can only guess, but she did, in fact, give the rebel leader the kiss he craved and, in turn, she was given the safe conduct across the heath and into London she had been promised.

Everything seemed to be going well for the rebels. When they marched towards the City, the Londoners lowered the drawbridge and gave them unchallenged access to London

Bridge. When they asked to meet the king, he rode out to meet
them.

Tyler and his lieutenants read their proposals to him, and
the king agreed to make them all free men and generally to
improve their lot.

It should have been a great popular victory from which the
Kent and Essex men could return home feeling that it had all
been very well worth while. But, unfortunately, as so often
happens, an unruly element permitted their euphoria to get
the better of them and a comparatively peaceful demonstration quickly turned into a riot of looting, plunder and murder.
That changed everything.

On June 17th, at a meeting at Smithfield, outside the city
walls, the young king again met his subjects and their leaders.
In a moment of loyal passion, William Walworth, Mayor of
London, drew a sword and stabbed Wat Tyler to death.

The king seized upon this moment with commendable opportunism and spurred his horse forward into the stunned mob.

'Your leader is dead!' he told them. 'Let me be your leader instead.'

Dispirited by the turn events had taken, the rebels meekly followed the king across London Bridge and out of the city. Once safely out of town, the freedom charters that had been promised them and, indeed, prepared for them, were torn up and 24 of them were executed. The rest went home, disillusioned and defeated.

The peasants revolt was over and the only character in the whole sorry drama to emerge with any credit was Princess Joan, the king's mother and beloved Fair Maid of Kent, who had understood the mood of the men sufficiently to entrust herself to them for no greater security than a royal kiss for the rebel leader.

Mrs Veal's
Ghost

G HOST stories abound in Kent, as indeed they do every-
where. Most of them are of quite local significance and
often the ghosts of one village are virtually unknown to its
neighbours.

A few, though, achieve wider notoriety for one reason or
another, as did the celebrated ghost of Mrs Veal, which was
the subject of a pamphlet by none other than Daniel Defoe,
and which aroused the interest of no less a person than Queen
Anne and her consort, Prince George of Denmark.

Mrs Veal lived in Dover, and one Saturday in 1705 she paid
a visit to an old friend of hers, Mrs Bargrave, in Canterbury.

The two old friends chatted together, catching up on all the
latest news and gossip of mutual friends and acquaintances,
and as the time neared for Mrs Veal to leave, she broached a
subject that somewhat surprised Mrs Bargrave.

'I wonder, my dear,' Mrs Veal asked, 'if you would do a
great favour for me? You see, I shall be going on a long
journey quite soon, and I can't do this for myself before I go.
What I would like is a gravestone made for my mother's
grave. Do you think you could arrange that for me?'

Mrs Bargrave was somewhat taken aback. It seemed a
strange thing for one friend to ask another, even on the eve of a
departure for a long journey. It was not at all the sort of favour
she had expected her friend to ask. But she said yes, of course,

51

if that was what Mrs Veal wanted, she would be happy to do it for her.

'Thank you so much,' said Mrs Veal. 'Nothing elaborate, you understand, but tasteful. I trust you. There is just one other thing, though . . . Would you instruct the stone mason to leave enough room on the stone, after he has inscribed it for my mother, for my own name to be added underneath. I would like to be buried in the same grave and to be remembered by the same stone, you see.'

This additional request presented no problem, so Mrs Bargrave agreed to that, too. 'But I'm sure there's no need for you to be thinking about a gravestone for yourself just yet,' she joked. 'I've never seen you looking in better health or sounding in better spirits than you are today.'

Mrs Veal smiled. 'Ah, well, you never know, do you?' she replied, and soon after took her leave, saying she was going to visit a cousin who also lived in Canterbury, while she was in the city.

Mrs Bargrave would not have given the request further thought had not word reached her that her friend Mrs Veal had died. She had died in Dover. And she had died the day before the two of them had talked together in Mrs Bargrave's parlour.

She was horrified and at first she thought there must have been some mistake. But inquiries persuaded her that there had not. Mrs Veal had, indeed, been lying dead in Dover on the day before her visit to Mrs Bargrave in Canterbury when she had ordered her own gravestone.

There was one inescapable conclusion to be drawn from that: it had not, in fact, been the healthy looking Mrs Veal who had chatted with Mrs Bargrave, but a ghost.

Mrs Bargrave could not keep such a thing to herself. Soon half Canterbury knew about the spectral visit and word spread beyond the city and reached the ears of the celebrated writer Daniel Defoe.

He made his own inquiries, recognised the commercial possibilities of such a story, and wrote a pamphlet about it, which was published under the all-embracing title: *A True Relation of the Apparition of one Mrs Veal, the next day after her death, to one Mrs Bargrave, at Canterbury, the 8th September, 1705 – which apparition recommends the Perusal of Drelincourt's Book of Consolations against the Fears of Death.*

Thanks to the pamphlet, the story claimed the attention of a number of members of high society and, in fact, found an audience at high society's very pinnacle when the Queen and her husband became interested. They arranged for the whole affair to be thoroughly investigated by some of the leading psychic researchers of their day.

Nothing they discovered, however, disproved Mrs Bargrave's story, and the tale was adopted, just as she and Mr Defoe had told it, into that volume of curious phenomena that make up the many tales of Old Kent.

Captain Swing

In the late summer of 1830 a Kent farmer received a letter which warned him that he was on the list of farmers and landowners marked down for the attentions of Captain Swing.

It was probably the most frightening letter he would ever receive. For Captain Swing was the most feared name in the county at the time – even though everyone knew there was no such man.

The name was adopted by farm labourers throughout Kent to disguise the identities of the gangs who went through the rural areas, firing ricks and barns and, in some cases, even houses. But they vented the worst of their fury on the farmers' threshing machines.

Times were hard for farm labourers in 1830. Ever since Wellington had ended the war with France at the Battle of Waterloo in 1815, British agriculture had wallowed in a long depression and the old mutual dependence and respect that had so characterised the relationship between English landowners and their workers in the 18th century had sunk into a widening gulf between rich and poor.

Most farm labourers were 'on the parish', receiving poor relief to supplement their meagre wages and provide their families with at least some of the greatest necessities of life. There were no signs that this state of affairs would ever change.

Indeed, the winter of 1829 had been the latest of a series of unusually hard ones in Kent and the hardships endured by ill-clothed, ill-fed families in their ill-heated homes were severe. When summer came at last, in 1830, there were many men who were ready to swear they would die in the attempt to achieve better conditions rather than face another winter like that one.

Low wages were at the heart of the trouble, although to a large extent the labourers did not blame the farmers for that. Often, the Captain Swing letters they delivered, usually at dead of night, urged a combined effort to force the government to reduce taxes and the generally detested church tithes, so that farmers could afford to pay their workers more. Some farmers responded by showing open sympathy with the men, though few actually joined with the labourers in their increasingly lawless behaviour as the summer wore on.

Throughout the country generally there was sympathy for

the plight of the poor. It was reflected in the defeat of the Conservative government in the General Election that year, and the installation of a Whig administration of which great reforms were expected. The outcome of that election had much to do with the popular mood that encouraged the rioting that broke out in Kent and spread to a score or more other counties in southern England that year.

In several of them, the leader the men acknowledged in public was the imaginary Captain Swing.

The men focused their attentions not on the farmers, but on their threshing machines. The machines did work that had once employed men through much of the worst of the winter, when the autumn harvest of grain was threshed indoors by the centuries-old methods of beating the ears of the corn with flails.

In some parishes, sympathetic landowners went so far as to advise their tenant farmers to stop using them and to go back to the old methods. Some farmers did. Some even dismantled their threshing machines so that they could not be used.

But most of the farmers hired the machines as they needed them and it was these, very often, that the gangs of machine-wreckers attacked, at first by night, but later in broad daylight. Sometimes farmers were warned of their coming by a Captain Swing letter, but often there was no more warning than that given by the spreading rumours of their coming.

The first threshing machine to be destroyed in the Captain Swing riots was at Lower Hardres, near Canterbury, on August 28th, 1830. That was a hired machine. Next day, another was destroyed some miles away at Newington, near Hythe. In both cases a gang of men from the village of Elham, with others from neighbouring villages, were held to be responsible.

By the third week, about 100 machines had been destroyed, most of them in East Kent. Some were battered into scrap by brute force and the biggest hammers their attackers could lay hands on. Others were skilfully dismantled. Often, a middle course brought blacksmiths, recruited out of sympathy or fear, to use their own special knowledge of machinery to do with a few well-aimed blows what less expert men would have taken much longer to achieve.

Seven men were charged with machine-breaking and tried at East Kent Sessions. They all pleaded guilty, but Sir Edward Knatchbull discharged them with a caution and a three-day prison sentence.

That same night, a machine was destroyed near Sittingbourne and the next day four more were rendered useless in the Canterbury area.

More men were brought to trial, but the magistrates who heard the cases themselves came under attack. Most of them were farmers or landowners, and they became the target for the threatening Captain Swing letters, and also for the rick and barn burning that accompanied the machine-breaking.

At Cranbrook, a troop of 25 dragoons had to be despatched to disperse a crowd that had gathered to protest against the machines and the conditions, and there were similar public meetings in other parts of Kent, too. Some of them were peaceful; some were not.

At many of these meetings, local men were elected to lead the protests, and were given complimentary ranks such as Captain or General, Lord or even, in one case at least, King. But it was the fictitious Captain Swing who signed the threatening letters.

The county was in a state of great excitement and there were all sorts of rumours: of revolutionary Frenchmen sneaking into Kent in the guise of smugglers and stirring up trouble where there had been none before; of known Radicals making improbably ubiquitous appearances in order to fuel the fires of unrest; of mysterious gentlemen dashing from one riotous assembly to another, always well-dressed and driving smart little horse-drawn gigs so that no-one should suspect that they were, in fact, professional rabble-rousers.

Even Methodist preachers came in for a share of the blame for what was going on and when William Cobbett (of *Rural Rides* fame) made a tour through Kent and Sussex that coincided with the outbreak of rioting, there was at least one rioter who, brought to court, told the Bench he had been incited to act as he had after hearing one of Cobbett's lectures.

Throughout the short and violent reign of Captain Swing, from 1830 until 1832, of prisoners tried by 12 different courts, 25 were acquitted, 4 were executed for arson, 48 were sentenced to varying terms of imprisonment and 52 were transported.

Moves for a general amnesty for the convicted rioters began almost as soon as their sentences were passed, but it was not until 1834 that the first of the Captain Swing convicts was pardoned and released. Those that had been transported were freed to return home, though few could raise the necessary fare to bring them back.

Historians differ about how effective the Swing riots of 1830 were. They did not immediately improve conditions for the labourers, although they did delay the introduction of threshing machines in the same sort of numbers for another twenty years which, after all, was the immediate aim of the men who destroyed them – the men who called themselves, collectively, Captain Swing.

St Augustine
and the
Nailbourne Stream

ONE of Kent's many beauty spots is the Elham Valley,
which takes its name from the lovely little village of
Elham, between Canterbury and Dover.

It is a place of sweeping hillsides and pretty, miniature
views, through which runs the celebrated Nailbourne stream.
The stream is spring-fed and, traditionally, it waters its course
only once every seven years.

That regularity is not entirely reliable but no-one begrudges
it a little licence in the matter. In any case, to question its
behaviour would be almost irreverent, in the circumstances,
for if tradition is to be believed this was a dry valley a
thousand years ago, in the days when St Augustine – then
simply Father Augustine – came to Kent.

Despite the familiar story that Augustine baptised Egbert,
King of Kent, at Easter and ten thousand of his subjects the
following Christmas, Kent did not abandon the old Saxon
gods easily. Even among those who were baptised, there were
many who embraced the new Christian religion as an addition
to, rather than a substitute for, their old beliefs, which
lingered on in the more rural areas for long after Augustine
was gone.

In several of the older Kent churches, there are still reminders of pagan influences, and there are customs still observed to this day which can be traced back to pre-Christian times, although their present-day observers do not always realise or acknowledge it.

Throughout his life in Kent, Augustine had always to be striving to drive the old ways deeper underground and to demonstrate, whenever he could, the greater benefits of Christianity. The Elham Valley Nailbourne stream was one such demonstration.

The story goes that the people of the valley were suffering particularly badly from a drought which was shrivelling their crops and parching their fields. They made all the customary pleas to the Old Gods to help them, but the gods withheld their help. The people were in despair.

In his abbey at Canterbury, Augustine heard about the plight of the people of the valley, and he rode out to see them and try to bring some comfort. When he arrived, he realised that they were in no condition to listen to his preaching. Words were not going to win them over. What they needed was action – specifically, action that would bring water to their unwatered lives.

So Augustine knelt and prayed to his God, asking Him to help these poor people. His prayers over, he stood up again and where he had been kneeling, a spring of clear water burst from the earth and began to flow in a stream through the valley.

The people, of course, were overjoyed. They were very impressed, too. Their prayers to their own gods had achieved nothing, yet this Holy Man had come among them and by his prayers had prevailed upon his God to give them the water they craved.

Augustine had no difficulty at all in persuading them to convert from their pagan ways and adopt the Christian faith.

But the Old Gods, although they had been deaf to the pleas of their own worshippers, were not blind to what was happening in what they regarded as strictly their own parish.

Angered, they conjured up a great storm which swept

through the valley, uprooting trees and causing havoc. The people wanted water, did they? Well now they had it. Plenty of it! They didn't need the pathetic little spring with which this interloper had sought to impress them, so they caused the storm to stop it up again, so that the water no longer flowed.

Then, having thus thwarted the efforts of Augustine and his God, they allowed the storm to abate and retired to see how the foreign holy man would handle this small demonstration of their own powers!

The local people, naturally, were not anxious to have the whole sequence of events repeated. They no longer doubted that Augustine could bring them water if he chose to, but if this was going to provoke the Old Gods into hurling trees about and flattening their crops, on the whole they reckoned they would be better off relying on the natural swings and roundabouts of good and bad seasons, just as they always had done.

But Augustine could not allow his God to be seen to have been defeated, so he prayed some more. Recognising the dilemma in which the local people found themselves, this time he asked that the Elham stream should flow, not all the time, but just once every seven years. That would be enough to overcome the effects of any intermediate droughts and relieve the worst of any suffering they might cause. It would also, in its own way, provide permanent evidence of the power of his God.

A stream that ran all the time would come to be taken for granted, but if it sprang from the earth only once every seven years, it would be a regular reminder to the people of the power that caused it to behave in such a very unconventional way.

The Old Gods, it seems, did not recognise the subtlety of this. They saw it as a victory for themselves and chose to be magnanimous enough to permit the arrangement.

So it was, according to tradition, that the Nailbourne stream flowed through the Elham valley once every seven years, a recurrent reminder that the Christian God was both more powerful and more wise than the old Saxon gods, who gradually lost favour and were abandoned.

As a matter of record, the Nailbourne does not flow always at the seventh year. But who is to say that, over the fullness of time through which it has and will fulfil its God-given destiny, its activity will not average out into seven-year cycles?

Nell Cook

ONE of the *Ingoldsby Legends* of Richard Barham is called
Nell Cook and it tells the story of what happened to the
young servant girl of a Friar at the Priory of St Saviour in
Canterbury in the time of King Henry VIII.

The Friar lived in a house near what is now known as The
Dark Entry – a narrow passage paved with flagstones leading
into the Cathedral cloisters and the crypt. He had a reputation
for indulgence that did not earn the approval of his more
abstemious brethren. His figure, they noted, belied reliance
upon the common fare of the Priory; his complexion hinted at
other refreshment than the weak beer from the refectory; and
his general manner was altogether more merry and worldly
than was becoming in a man of his calling.

Much of this uncharacteristic well-being was generally
supposed to be to the credit of his cook, a young woman called
Ellen Bean who, for reasons that no doubt contented him well
enough, the Canon chose to call Nell Cook.

Nell was famous for her cooking. It was said she could make
a banquet out of old shoes, although there is no evidence that
she was ever called upon to do so. But she was also renowned
within the Precincts, if not beyond, for being a particularly
pretty young woman, and there were those among the monks
and in the town who wondered if it was entirely necessary –
indeed, if it was even right – for a Clerk in Holy Orders to
have, living in the same house with him, quite such a pretty
cook.

However, one Whitsun there arrived at the Friar's house a

to fire her jealousy to action at last. At the earliest opportunity, she went out to buy ingredients for a rather special dish she proposed to cook for the Friar and his 'niece'. That night, she sent up for his supper one of her famous Warden Pies.

Next day, when the monks gathered for morning prayer, it was remarked that the Friar did not join them. It was so exceptional for him to absent himself from his devotions that a search was made throughout the Cathedral and the Precincts. Nell was questioned, of course, but she swore she had no idea where her master was. Finally, they searched the house, eventually breaking open the door to his room, and there they found the Friar and his 'niece' together. Both were dead.

The monks were horrified. The discovery threatened a scandal which had to be avoided at all costs. A midnight funeral service was held and the Friar and the lady were laid to rest, side by side, in a grave dug specially in the Cathedral nave.

However, from the moment of the scandalous discovery, Nell Cook disappeared. Inquiries were made about her among the monks but they all declined to speculate about where she might be. For some years afterwards the fate of Nell Cook remained a total mystery.

Then, one day a flagstone in the Dark Entry became loose, and three masons were called in to fix it. They lifted the stone and found themselves peering down into a small cavity in which huddled a skeleton. Near the bones was a dish containing a mouldy piece of crust from a Warden Pie.

The bones were examined and declared to be those of a female. The mystery of the disappearance of Nell Cook was generally thought to have been solved at last. It was supposed that, determined to keep secret the misbehaviour of their Friar, and at the same time punish Nell for poisoning him, the monks had entombed Nell under the paving stone, alive, with a piece of her own fatal Warden Pie, which she could either eat and poison herself, or refuse and starve to death.

After that, it was said that the ghost of Nell Cook walked the

Dark Entry regularly every Friday night and that whoever saw her was doomed to die within the year.

Why? Because the first victims of the ghost were none other than the three masons who lifted the flagstone that had sealed the mortal remains of Nell into her tomb and, presumably, released her vengeful spirit into the Dark Entry. All three of them, the story ended, died within the year – two of them hanged for murdering the third!

Father Wilson
and the
Little Hoppers

THE village of Five Oak Green, some four miles from
Tonbridge, is fairly undistinguished as Kent villages go,
being neither specially picturesque nor blessed with famous
associations. Yet it has one feature that makes it unique
among Kent's villages, and that is the site of the former Little
Hoppers' Hospital.

The Hospital is no more, now. Thankfully, the little hoppers for whom it was provided are no more either. But a
century ago, Five Oak Green was one of those Weald of Kent
villages to which flocked, every year, hundreds of migrant
hop-pickers.

For this was the heart of the Kentish hop-growing region
and throughout the 19th century and the beginning of the
20th, thousands of people from some of the poorest districts of
London came to find seasonal work in the hop gardens.

One of the characteristics of traditional hop growing was
that the hundreds of acres, producing thousands of tons of
hops, all had to be harvested in three of four weeks at the end
of the summer, usually in September.

All through the 18th and 19th centuries, Kent was the
premier hop-growing county in England and farmers had to

rely on the Londoners to augment local labour to get the hops picked in time.

Once, the migrants used to walk from their homes in London to the hop gardens in Kent. Later, when the railways reached out into the countryside, special trains were provided and the 'hoppers' (as they were always called) left London very early in the morning in enormous numbers, men, women and children, crowding on to the terminal platforms and into the trains which brought them at special cheap fares through the dawning day to places like Tonbridge and Paddock Wood.

There, they were disgorged into the villages, while most of the villagers were still having their breakfasts, to await collection by horse and cart (if they were lucky) and taken to the surrounding farms with which the various parties were booked to work.

At the farms they were allotted places in barns and cart sheds or old army tents, where they huddled together on earth floors covered with straw for their living spaces.

If the season was good, and the weather was fine, it was something of a holiday, with pay, for many of the hoppers. Conditions on the farms were appalling by modern standards, but for many of the Londoners it was no worse – in some ways, better – than their normal living conditions throughout the rest of the year, even though, if it was wet, many of them literally lived in wet clothes and slept on wet and rotting straw for days or even weeks at a time.

It was no wonder then, that there were epidemics of cholera, typhus and all sorts of other diseases and illnesses. Many of the Londoners went home at the end of the hopping to die of lung infections and other complaints contracted or aggravated by their 'holiday' in Kent.

Most of the Kent pickers came from the South London boroughs, including Stepney where one of the priests was Father Richard Wilson of St Augustine's.

Father Wilson had seen the hordes of hoppers leaving his parish year after year without wondering very much about what they were going to. He knew they went to work in the fields in Kent, but that was all. When his curiosity was aroused, however, he questioned some of his flock about what it was like, this hop picking that emptied the parish every year. The answer he got was not specially helpful. 'Hopping', came the frequently repeated answer, 'is hell!'

So Father Wilson decided he must find out for himself just what sort of hell it was to which these people migrated so regularly, and in 1896 he persuaded one of the families to allow him to go with them.

That was how he came to join the great exodus of people and their belongings – often they took virtually all they possessed, including bedding, pots and pans, piled on hand-carts and old prams or packed into tin baths which two of the children carried between them – that crowded into the hoppers' specials at London Bridge Station.

The train took him to Paddock Wood and from there the family Father Wilson travelled with walked to a farm near Five Oak Green. The priest settled down for the duration of the season with the unmarried men, who were housed in a barn.

It was usual for the unmarried men to be segregated from the women on arrival. It was also very common for the segregation to be ignored after the first day or two!

For the whole of that season, Father Wilson picked hops with his chosen family, watching and listening and learning all he could about just what his parishioners meant when they spoke of 'hopping down in Kent'.

Much that he saw horrified him. The only drinking water for the whole camp was drawn as it was needed from a dirty farm pond. The only lavatories were the nearest ditch – which drained into the same pond. Each family did its own cooking on its own camp fire – if the weather was good enough. If it wasn't, then no cooking was done, no water was heated. Once, the priest saw a man's dead body left lying covered with sacks in a ditch.

But most important for the future was his chance meeting one day with a woman who was carrying a brown paper

70

parcel. He asked her what was in the parcel and she told him it was the dead body of her baby, which she had carried five miles to a doctor only to be told when she got there that the child was already dead. Father Wilson was shocked and vowed to make sure, if he could, that such a thing never happened again.

The following year he returned to Five Oak Green, not with one of the hopper families this time, but with three volunteer nurses. They hired a cottage for two and sixpence a week and there they set up the first Little Hoppers' Hospital, where the sick children of the hop-pickers could be taken in and looked after properly.

That first year there was an epidemic of smallpox and Father Wilson and his nurses were kept very busy throughout the hop-picking season. They could not meet more than a fraction of the need, but at the end of the season it was clear to them all that the need was, indeed, a desperate one. It was decided that the hospital should be a continuing service for as long as it was necessary.

The next year, Father Wilson was back again, this time in a larger rented cottage. It still was not big enough to cope with all the little patients that were brought to him.

At last, in 1910, he was able to move into an old disused public house, the Rose and Crown at Five Oak Green, where the former wooden skittles alley was equipped as the first real children's ward. In 1927 that was replaced by a purpose-built brick building, which became the Richard Wilson Memorial. It was known throughout the Weald of Kent as The Little Hoppers' Hospital.

Father Wilson was not the only, nor indeed the first, of the reformers who fought for better conditions for the hoppers. But he became trusted by farmers and pickers alike in the Paddock Wood area, and was able to contribute significantly, not only to the treatment of the children in his hospital, but also to the gradual changes that came in the way the hoppers were treated.

It was he who introduced the London British Red Cross

71

Society to the Five Oak Green area, and it was his work and the publicity it received that brought several of the University College missions to the hop gardens to extend the work he had begun.

The Little Hoppers' Hospital did valuable work for years, up to and including the Second World War. After that, though, the numbers of migrant workers declined. Much improved social conditions in London meant that the Londoners were no longer keen to spend working holidays in the Kentish hop gardens, even though conditions there, too, were very much better than they had been when Father Wilson made his first trip to Kent.

The farmers had to introduce the new hop picking machines which were already being used very successfully in America, to take the place of the 'hoppers'. Very soon, the machines had ousted the workers almost entirely.

Now, apart from a few, mostly students and local people, who look after the machines, hop-picking is virtually entirely mechanised. The Father Wilson memorial is still there, though, identified by a sign over the entrance to the building, but it is a hospital no longer.

Thankfully, there is never likely to be a need for a Little Hoppers' Hospital anywhere in Kent again.

The
Lost Bells
of Newington

THE village of Newington lies just off the A2 London–
Dover road near Sittingbourne and is renowned for
nothing very much – apart from the tale that the Devil once
stole its church bells.

This story originated several hundred years ago, when the
bells in the tower of the church at Newington were, in fact,
stolen. It seems quite likely that they were actually stolen by
the church wardens, probably to be melted down and sold for
the value of the metal.

But what village would want to be noted for its thieving
church wardens? Newington reburnished its tarnished reputation rather ingeniously, by spreading the word that what had
really happened was that the Devil had become so incensed by
the joyful sound of the bells while he was trying to get some
sleep one Sunday, that he resolved that the bells would have to
go.

One night, the story goes, he took a sack and climbed up to
the bell chamber where he took down the bells and put them
into the sack. Then, impatient to dispose of his troublesome
booty, he jumped down from the tower.

At that time there were two large sarsen stones standing

together not far from the church, and as he jumped down, the Devil landed on one of the stones, stumbled and fell.

It was this misfortune that provided the village with the evidence to support its story, because as the Prince of Darkness stumbled over the stone, he left on it the imprint of his booted foot.

Of course, it is well-known that the Devil never wears boots, and that one of the ways in which his many disguises may be penetrated by mortal observation is through the give-away cloven hoof he can never conceal, whatever other changes he makes to his appearance.

Newington's answer to this was that the second of the two stones bore the unmistakable imprint of just such a cloven hoof – right up to the time it disappeared from the local scene, none could say how or when!

As further proof of the truth of its local legend, the village went on to assert that, as he stumbled and fell the bells spilled out of the sack and went rolling away into a nearby stream, where they were lost for ever.

No doubt the Devil limped back to his infernal rest, content that a somewhat clumsy night's work had, nevertheless, rid him of those tiresome Newington bells at last.

The good people of Newington, however, were loth to accept that their bells had gone for good. They consulted the local witch about the whole matter, and she told them that the bells would only be recovered if the stream was dragged by four pure white cows.

Well, it took the villagers a long time to get together a team of four pure white cows, but such was their determination to have their bells back and pealing again that they eventually did it. They harnessed the animals to the drag and set to work to recover their beloved bells.

For some reason, though, it was not as easy as they had been led to suppose it would be. Over and over again the drag caught on something below the surface of the stream and began to pull it up. Each time, before it broke the surface, however, the object fell back again.

The villagers were quite convinced that they were close to success, and they could not understand why their efforts were being thwarted in this way.

At last, a small boy who had been standing on the bank of the stream watching, drew attention to the fact that he alone had noticed: the cows were not pure white all over, as the witch had said they must be.

One of the villagers took a closer look at the cows and found that, sure enough, not one of the four was as pure white as they had all believed them to be. Each one had a small black mark which no-one had noticed – except the boy – until that moment.

So that was that! The men abandoned the task and all hope of ever recovering their church bells, which were allowed to rest in peace at the bottom of the stream.

The two stones with the Devil's footprints on them, one booted, the other not, remained where they were at what came to be known as Devil's Corner for many years after that. Then, in 1935, by which time the one with the cloven hoof imprinted on it had disappeared, probably broken up by local builders, the remaining stone with the booted imprint was moved.

It was uprooted from its old site, where it had become something of a traffic hazard, and repositioned near the churchyard. It was, after all, by now a noted local curiosity and a convenient reminder to sceptics who doubted the origin and the nature of the bootprint, that the Devil is abroad in the world still, even if he rarely steals church bells nowadays.

But as soon as the stone was removed, local people began to notice a whole series of small but tiresome misfortunes afflicting the village and its people. They urged the parish council to order the stone to be put back where it came from before something really bad happened.

For a little while, there was quite a local to-do about it, but the parish councillors took a worldly view of the whole matter and, after a while, Newington settled down again and was no more unfortunate than any other village.

Less than some, in fact, because it isn't every village that can point to hard evidence that it once had a visit from no less a Person than His Satanic Majesty himself!

St Bartholomew's Day Battle

IF you go to the old Kent town and port of Sandwich you will certainly be invited to see St Bartholomew's Chapel on the outskirts of the town. The chapel, with its cluster of alms-houses round a small rectangular courtyard, is attractive enough in itself, but it is made all the more interesting by association with the colourful story that is told about how it originated, 700 years ago.

It began when the French Dauphin, Louis, was invited to invade England by the barons during their dispute with King John. Not everyone welcomed him, and one of those that did not was Hubert de Burgh, the Constable of Dover Castle.

Louis demanded the surrender of the castle, and when it was denied him he laid siege to it. Hubert, however, sent a message to Louis saying: 'Never will I yield to French aliens this castle, which is the very key and gate of England!'

This was fighting talk if ever Louis heard it, and he had to admit that if Dover Castle was not surrendered to him there was no way he was going to be able to take it by force. In the end, he had to give up the attempt and retire back to France.

Six months later he was back again. This time, instead of besieging Dover he landed at Sandwich, which he burned and then made preparations for a march on London just as soon as his French fleet of reinforcements and supplies could join him from across the Channel.

That fleet was also heading for Sandwich, a natural thing to do in those days when the town was the premier south of England port and possibly the premier port of all England.

Most of the Sandwich boats had been destroyed by the Dauphin's raiders, leaving only three of them intact in the harbour. The men of the Cinque Ports were not at their best for fighting off invaders, and morale in Sandwich was very low. Not only had the Portsmen been pretty soundly trounced by the Dauphin, but word had reached them that the French fleet was under the command of Eustace, a renegade monk who was notorious on both sides of the Channel for being a dabbler in the Black Arts and for being endowed with supernatural powers.

One way and another, the Kent men felt that the odds seemed to be pretty unequally stacked against them.

As they stood on the quayside and watched the French sails littering the horizon, heading towards them, they felt their best hope lay in prayer and, it being St Bartholomew's Day (August 24th) 1217, they directed their prayers in his direction, reminding the saint that they had long paid him the homage due to him on this day every year and suggesting that present circumstances offered him a very good opportunity to show his appreciation by coming to their aid.

Being very practical men and fully understanding that in this life no-one, not even saints, could be expected to do something for nothing, they promised that, if he would take notice of their prayers and use his influence to swing things their way in the coming unequal battle, they would raise enough money to build a chapel which they would dedicate specially to him.

Now, whether or not the saint had anything to do with it, there was among the Sandwich men that day one called Stephen Crabbe, who told his townsfolk that he knew Eustace the Monk quite well.

'In fact,' he said, 'I was once his pupil and I know some of the dark secrets for which this renegade is renowned.'

To support what he said, he pointed out something that

none of the others had noticed up to this moment: that although the French fleet was now in plain view, the ship in which Eustace sailed was not. That, Master Crabbe explained, was because the magician had rendered it, complete with himself and his crew, invisible.

The Portsmen very nearly turned tail there and then. But Crabbe rallied them by assuring them that having him with them put them at no disadvantage whatever since he was more than a match for the French monk.

'He is invisible to you – but not to me,' he told them. 'I will employ the same sort of magic he uses, and so we shall defeat him on his own terms. Come on, lads: let's go get 'em!' (Or, at any rate, 13th century Kentish words to that effect.)

So putting their trust in St Bartholomew and Stephen Crabbe, the men of Sandwich launched their three remaining ships and headed for the oncoming French fleet, taking Master Crabbe with them aboard one of the ships.

However, before they left the harbour they loaded their ships with bins of quicklime, reckoning that, in all the circumstances, the normal though scant chivalries of sea warfare could be suspended for the day. Instead of carrying out the customary tactics of coming directly alongside the enemy ships and swarming aboard, hacking down as many of their crew as they could, this time they first manoeuvred their ships to windward of the invasion fleet.

As soon as they were in a favourable position, they tossed quicklime into the air so that it was carried into the eyes of the Frenchmen, blinding them so that they were quite unable to defend themselves when the Englishmen boarded.

It worked splendidly, although, of course, the Portsmen could not be sure the French flagship with Eustace aboard had been disabled like the others, because they still could not see it. Stephen Crabbe, however, had no hesitation in piloting the ship in which he sailed close to where he promised Eustace was and, at the right moment, he leaped from the deck of his own ship into the invisible one alongside and began laying about him with his sword, much to the astonishment of the rest of the crew, to whose eyes he appeared to be floating in the air a few feet above the surface of the sea.

While they were still making up their minds whether or not they should follow him, Crabbe hacked his way to where the invisible Eustace stood on an invisible deck and with a mighty slice of his sword cut off the Frenchman's head.

At once, the French ship became visible. Perhaps, in that moment of triumph, Crabbe lost his concentration. Or perhaps all the hacking that had gone into reaching Eustace had taken its toll. Whatever the reason, moments after the monk's head fell, the remaining members of the French crew fell upon Crabbe and killed him. They cut the body to pieces and threw the bits overboard into the sea.

The men of Sandwich watched his end in dismay. They had been on the very brink of launching themselves into a victorious foray, but now they hesitated once more.

At that moment, though, who should appear among them, dressed in distinctive red garments to make sure he was seen and recognised, but St Bartholomew himself. He caused a great squall to blow up, and this capsized the French ships, although the smaller English ships were unaffected. Abruptly, the battle was over, and the Portsmen were left victorious.

The Sandwich men turned their ships and sailed back home. They were very grateful to the saint, and did not forget their promise. They built the chapel and dedicated it to St Bartholomew. Then, just to show that there was nothing niggardly about Kentish gratitude, they built the adjoining almshouses, too. They also allotted enough local land to support the chapel and the almshouses for ever.

Sandwich still has its St Bartholomew's Chapel. It still has its almshouses. But, more to the present point, it has never forgotten the story of how the Portsmen defeated the French in the St Bartholomew's Day Battle of Sandwich.

Canterbury
Fair

F OR centuries, in towns and cities all over England, the
annual fair was a time to look forward to for weeks before
the event and to remember for months afterwards. Even 200
years ago, a day at the fair was an exciting highlight in the
lives of many people, who gladly walked ten or fifteen miles to
experience it.

All the major towns and many of the smaller ones, too, held
their annual fairs. Some were held for a specific purpose, like
the hiring fairs at which labourers offered themselves for hire
for the coming year.

If a man was dissatisfied with the work he was doing or,
more often, the man he was doing it for, he would dress
himself in his best clothes and present himself at the hiring
fair. A carter would carry his long carter's whip; a ploughman
would carry a 'shining stick' – a wand of peeled willow; and a
shepherd would wear a piece of sheep's fleece either in his hat
or pinned to his coat or smock. By a variety of such traditional
and easily recognised badges men with experience of particu-
lar work would signify their willingness to accept offers of
employment.

A good man, who believed he was worth more, either in pay
or conditions, than he was currently getting from his master,
might attract several offers during the course of a day at the
fair. Some, whose reputations were well-known, might even

81

have prospective employers bidding against each other for their services, and might then end up by going back to the man they had quit, their dissatisfaction publicly aired and the belief in their greater worth thoroughly vindicated.

Others, of course, who had been unable to keep one job, not necessarily through any fault of their own, might end the day having to accept any offer made to them.

There were horse fairs, sheep fairs, goose fairs, fruit and other produce fairs, and the main object of them all was to advertise wares or services for sale.

They were also a rare opportunity to buy things. The fairs brought together farmers and villagers from miles around and were occasions for renewing pots and pans, baskets and clothing, furnishings and all sorts of other domestic necessities, as well as 'fairings' – souvenirs of the great day out.

They were social occasions, as well. People who only met annually or even less often at the fair, caught up with all the news and gossip and, of course, it was a splendid opportunity for the lads and lasses to meet others of their own age. Many a wedding resulted from a first meeting at a fair.

Some marriages ended there, too. In a time when divorce was almost unknown, certainly among the lower reaches of the social pyramid, a man might take his wife to the fair to sell her.

Usually, the transaction was not quite as casually commercial as that sounds. Often the 'sale' was pre-arranged, with a wayward wife being 'bought' by a man who was already her lover.

One of the most celebrated of the fairs held in Kent was the Michaelmas (September) fair at Canterbury. That was a hiring fair, and it was the subject of a famous Kent dialect poem, a hundred four-line verses long, called *Dick and Sal at Canterbury Fair*. It tells the story of a day at the fair for bailiff's boy Dick and a girl who was possibly his wife Sal, although elsewhere in the narrative it seems more likely that she was, in fact, his sister.

All Canterbury was thronged with people for the week-long

fair and the poem tells of the adventures of the young couple as they gawped their rustic way through the city in search of the fairground, where they bought six penn'orth of nuts, watched a donkey race with cheeses for prizes, took part in races and generally enjoyed the fun of the fair, where there were all sorts of amusements and entertainments, including roundabouts and swing-boats.

Before they left, they bought a book, a new gown for Sal and a ribbon for her hair, to take home with them as mementoes of their day.

The poem ends with their departure from Canterbury at seven o'clock in the evening to begin the long walk home, probably (although it is not named) to the village of Sheldwich, some ten miles away.

We get some idea of just how much of an attraction the fair was when we realise that this couple walked twenty miles, there and back, and were on their feet most of the day while they were in Canterbury, too, and counted it well worth while. What stupendous event would be necessary today that would spur a couple to such efforts in order to be present?

Gianetta
A Love Story

THE great house of Knole at Sevenoaks is one of Kent's most stately of stately homes. Now owned by the National Trust, it was for centuries the home of the Sackville family and is famous for having 7 courtyards (one for each day of the week), 52 staircases (one for each week of the year) and 365 rooms (one for each day of the year).

Vita Sackville-West, the writer, whose home it was when she was a child, threw some doubt upon that tradition, but it persists nevertheless, even if it isn't quite literally correct.

In any case, however many old rooms, staircases and court-yards there are, it is a lovely old house which has been owned by archbishops and monarchs, has welcomed a galaxy of distinguished guests over the centuries, and is still enjoyed by thousands of less distinguished if not less worthy ones today.

There are a great many stories told about the house and its owners, but none of them, perhaps, is more eloquently re-called than the piquant love story of John Sackville, 3rd Duke of Dorset, and his lovely ballerina, Gianetta Baccelli.

The Duke was young; he inherited the title when he was only twenty-four. He was handsome, influential and very rich, and he had had several mistresses before 1783 when he was sent to become English Ambassador at the Court of Versailles in France. He was said to be a man who treated the women who loved him with an easy heartlessness which failed to diminish their affection for him, and it was rumoured that it was not long after he arrived in France that he became one of the lovers of Marie Antoinette herself.

In one of his despatches to the Foreign Office, he wrote: 'It is hardly possible to conceive a moment of more perfect tranquillity than the present.' This does not say very much for his Ambassadorial perspicacity, since he wrote it only three years before the Bastille was stormed and the French Revolution erupted.

Nevertheless, he obviously enjoyed himself in Paris. He did not like the French, he said, but they clearly liked him well enough. Their appreciation of his qualities may well have been enhanced a great deal by his boast that he spent about £11,000 a year, much of it on entertaining. He mixed freely in French, English and Italian society and particularly enjoyed the company of singers and actors and bohemian types generally. One of those who quickly captivated him, as she had many others, was the ballet dancer Gianetta Baccelli.

She was beautiful, clever, talented and, like him, she enjoyed flouting the polite conventions of the time. Once, after he gave her his Order of the Garter, with a *Honi Soit Qui Mal Y Pense* motto picked out in diamonds, she wore it as a headband on stage during one of her performances.

After he brought her home with him to Knole, he scandalised Kent society by sending her to a ball one evening wearing the Sackville family jewels.

At Knole, he installed her in her own suite of rooms above the Bourchier Gatehouse – the gatehouse built by Archbishop Bourchier after he bought the house in 1456. The gateway separates the Green Court from the Stone Court and has two small turrets, one of which is known as Shelley's Tower.

It is, in fact, only an enclosed staircase leading to the rooms in which Giannetta lived and Shelley is the name given it by Kentish servants who could not be bothered with difficult foreign names and preferred their own abbreviated pronunciation of Boccelli.

It was to these apartments that John would come, probably

by way of the Shelley Tower staircase, to spend his nights of
love with his ballerina. The couple caused something of a stir,
even in society that delighted in scandalous behaviour. He
had her portrait painted by both Gainsborough and Sir
Joshua Reynolds, and he also had a likeness of her sculpted,
nude, lying face down on a bed of carved silken covers, her
hair adorned by a single rose in a ribbon, one long and shapely
leg resting lightly upon the other.

The liaison lasted six years, during which they had several
children, all but one of which died while still babies. The
survivor grew up and went to school in Sevenoaks, but was
thereafter lost to history.

Then, in 1789, a newspaper announcement told the world:
'The Duke of Dorset and the Baccelli have just separated.' It
added: 'She is said to have behaved very well!'

In fact, it seems it was probably a fairly amicable parting,
which both accepted as inevitable. They had never married
and the *affaire* had lasted much longer and been more con-
stant than Gianetta could have hoped it would when she first
came to Knole.

The following year, the Duke married heiress Arabella
Diana Cope. One contemporary referred to 'her person,

though not feminine, might be denominated handsome and, if her mind was not highly cultivated or informed, she could boast of intellectual endowments that fitted her for the active business of life'.

Perhaps her £140,000 dowry was some compensation for her lack of the qualities the Baccelli had had in such abundance. Where Gianetta had been beautiful, compliant, witty and amusing, Arabella was severe and orderly. Soon the duke had turned from his early extravagances and become fretful and quarrelsome.

Dutifully, his duchess bore him three children – which was, after all, the object of their marriage. But she also banished the beautiful nude statue of Gianetta to one of the Knole attics. One wonders if the duke ever sneaked away to spend a little while with the most tangible memorial to his youth that remained at Knole during his increasingly morose maturity.

He died in 1799, aged 54, leaving his wife one of the richest and most politically influential widows this country has ever had, and his descendants a beautiful reminder in stone of the woman he always loved.

The Battle
of Maidstone

THE full fury of the Civil War did not break in Kent until June 1648, when Royalists and Parliamentarians fought hand to hand in the county town of Maidstone.

Before that year, Kent had remained Royalist and relatively peaceful in spite of a series of petitions and protests to Parliament. As early as 1642, some of the gentry of Kent had drawn up a petition urging the Parliamentarians to reach some sort of agreement with King Charles I so that the people could know whose orders should be obeyed, those of Parliament or those of the King.

The petition was drawn up in the name of the Maidstone Assize for West Kent, but fear of Parliamentary reaction limited its signatories to 19. The rest no doubt felt their judgment had been sound when Parliament committed the presiding judge, Sir Thomas Mallett, to the Tower for not having opposed it.

Nevertheless, support for the petition grew after that until at last it was sufficiently well-backed for it to be presented to Parliament by Richard Lovelace.

Parliament took it very badly and Lovelace was clapped into prison. Here, incidentally, he wrote his famous poem *To Althea, from prison*, the last verse of which begins with his best-known lines: 'Stone walls do not a prison make, Nor iron bars a cage . . .'

When the Maidstone Assize assembled next, in July 1642, Parliament sent a committee of 17 of its members to administer the county. The Assize objected most strongly to this and there was a stormy meeting. At the end of it a group of young Royalists drew up a formal protest and stated they were ready to put forward a proposal that could serve as the basis for a settlement of the differences between King and Parliament.

A copy of this petition was sent to Charles I at York, who replied with a promise of his protection for the petitioners. The petition was duly presented to Parliament also and it reacted by summoning some of the authors to London and confiscating their estates as surety for the huge fines they were told they would have to pay.

In that year of frustration there were several unsuccessful attempts to organise risings in Kent, but although there were many Royalist supporters in the county, generally life remained peaceful. A county committee was set up by Parliament to govern the county, as happened elsewhere, and the unrest simmered quietly beneath the surface during the following five years of the Civil War. Then, in 1647, Parliament banned religious festivals.

When the people of Canterbury realised that included in the ban was the entire festival of Christmas they rebelled openly, in what came to be called the Plum Pudding Riots.

Parliamentary soldiers put down the Canterbury riots, arresting several prominent ringleaders, but when the defendants came for trial the jury refused to return a verdict, saying the charges were invalid.

By now the whole of Kent was in a distinctly rebellious mood, urged on by Royalists who had been out of the county fighting for the King and who had returned home following his defeat, still eager to carry on the struggle in any way they could.

Another Royalist petition was prepared, urging Parliament to make peace with the King, to disband the army and to reduce taxation. A mass meeting was held on Blackheath, and here support for the petition was sufficient to encourage the petitioners to emerge into open revolt. A committee of gentry was formed, weapons were seized, towns and castles all around the county were taken over.

Efforts to negotiate a peaceful outcome failed and Parliament decided it had to enforce its will upon Kent with the help of the army.

The Royalists, led by the Earl of Norwich, mustered 10,000 men on Penenden Heath, on the northern edge of Maidstone, and there they prepared to meet the Parliamentary army under General Fairfax.

He had about 70,000 men, but he split his force and sent only a small part of it directly towards Penenden Heath. The Earl of Norwich was misled into advancing to meet it, and as this happened, Fairfax led the rest of his men round Maidstone to the south, across the River Medway and into an attack on Maidstone from the rear.

The people of Maidstone defended their town doggedly. They felled trees across the roads and dug ditches in the path of the oncoming army. They brought up cannons and posted snipers behind hedges and in buildings along the route Fairfax's men must come, to slow their advance.

But they could not stop them and during the evening of June 1st, 1648, in pouring rain, the Battle of Maidstone was fought. The townsfolk did their best and the Parliamentary victory was not easily won. But they were decisively outnumbered, and out-soldiered because by the time Norwich realised he had been tricked into marching away from the town and had turned hurriedly back to meet the real attack, it was too late to save the town.

The battle lasted about five hours and soon after midnight the Parliamentarians were coping with the last of the defenders. Historians differ about quite where that last stand was made, but they agree it was probably in one or other of the town's churchyards.

The Royalists lost 300 men killed and about 1,500 taken prisoner, as well as a small arsenal of weapons. The Parliamentary losses of men were about the same, but it was claimed as a major victory and thanksgiving services were held in London churches when the news of the outcome of the battle reached the city.

Fairfax marched his army around Kent for a few months more, ending at Sandown Castle which he captured on 5th September. With its fall, the Kentish rising ended.

In November 1648 a Parliamentarian, Andrew Broughton, was elected Mayor of Maidstone. He later distinguished himself by attending the trial of Charles I and reading the sentence of death that was passed on the King. With the return of the monarchy in 1660, though, he deemed it prudent to flee the country and he lived out the rest of his life in Switzerland.

The Pantiles
at
Tunbridge Wells

THE Pantiles at Tunbridge Wells is today described as the perfect pedestrian precinct. Certainly, it is one of the most attractive features of Kent's newest town.

It was a Royal accident that bequeathed The Pantiles to the town, just as it was a London lord's over-indulgence that gave the town to Kent in the first place.

Where Tunbridge Wells lies today, right on the south west edge of Kent, was nothing but open heath and woods 300 years ago. In 1606 Dudley, 3rd Baron North, was obeying doctor's orders and taking a rest from his hectic round of London's social life at the hunting lodge of his friend, Lord Bergavenny, at Eridge, in Sussex.

Healthy it may well have been there; lively it certainly was not, and Lord North soon decided he might just as well die happy in the thick of London's high life as live miserably in the rustic boredom of rural England.

It was as he set off towards London again that he noticed a pool in a wood. He had been worried about his health for some time and had toured some of the Continental spas in search of relief from the consequences of over-indulgence, and he recognised the rusty colour of the pool as similar to what he had seen in one of the German spas.

He borrowed a cup from a nearby cottager and drank some of the water. It tasted like the German spa water, too. So he put some into a bottle and took it back to London with him, to have it analysed.

Analysis confirmed his belief that what he had was mineral-rich water from a chalybeate spring, and so he went back to Eridge the following year and began to drink the water regularly. He was so pleased with the results that he told all his friends about the 'miracle cure' he had discovered, and soon fashionable people were making the 40-mile journey from London to Lord North's well.

In fact, enough of them began to arrive to make it worth the while of Lord Bergavenny, on whose estate the pond was, to clear the trees, sink a well and pave the area around it, so that the season's high fashion footwear did not suffer too badly from nature in the raw.

That is all that was done, though. Even when Henrietta Maria, Queen of Charles I, came to the well in 1630 as part of her recuperation following the birth of the future Charles II, there was nowhere nearby for her to stay, and she and her retinue had to camp out in tents on the common land.

Still, it couldn't have been too bad for her. She stayed six weeks and was said to be 'much improved' when she went back to London at the end of that time.

The nearest town to the well was Tonbridge (then spelled Tunbridge) some five or six miles away on the river Medway, and so it was natural that the well became known as Tunbridge Wells. The spelling persisted even after Tonbridge changed its first vowel.

The Royal patronage increased the popularity of the place enormously, and in 1636 the growing number of visitors, who still had to camp out on the common or find lodgings in Tonbridge or elsewhere and travel daily to take the water, were provided with a pipe house for the gentlemen and a coffee house for the ladies.

93

The area was levelled and a double row of elm and lime trees was planted, creating walks where The Quality could parade to see and be seen.

Very soon, countryfolk and tradesmen were setting up stalls in the walks, and musicians arrived to form a regular band for the entertainment of the visitors. Houses were built. Gradually, amid the rural scene that was so much a feature of the place, a town began to grow.

It prospered and soon had its own season, just as Bath and other fashionable resorts had. This lasted from May to October, and the court of Charles II regularly removed itself from London to Tunbridge Wells for the summer. Indeed, by the 1660s, Tunbridge Wells was one of the major resorts and was particularly famous for its informality. Tradesmen and nobles mingled freely and both joined in the country dances that were held there.

Soon shops and coffee houses had ousted the stalls. A colonnade was built to give shelter to shoppers and promenaders when it rained and London traders opened shops in Tunbridge Wells and brought their wares to where many of their customers were throughout the summer.

At this time the Walks were still unpaved and when the future Queen Anne brought her son, the Duke of Gloucester, there in 1698, the child slipped on the Upper Walk and cut his knee. Anne, who had already donated several generous sums of money to pay for improvements to the town and its entertainments, at once gave £100 to have the surface paved properly, for the greater comfort and safety of all who used it.

When she returned the following year, though, she found the money had been spent on other things and the work was not done. Deeply offended, she left the town in a high dudgeon, declaring she would never set foot in the place again.

She never did, either, even though the local people clubbed together to raise the money to have the paving carried out forthwith.

The work was done with pan-tiles – square clay tiles laid on the bare ground. The name stuck, and although most of the tiles were replaced with Purbeck stone slabs at the end of the 18th century, the area is still known as The Pantiles to this day, and is still lined with colonnaded shops.

There is still a band-stand there, where musical concerts and open air performances of other kinds are given from time to time. Trees still line the pavements, and it is still possible to sample the bitter tasting water from the well.

There is still, too, an air of other-timeness about The Pantiles which attracts thousands of visitors every year to browse among the book shops, antique shops, boutiques and restaurants, and to tread safely where once a Royal prince fell over and cut his knee.